WESTMINSTER SCHOOLS

PRESENTED BY

SMYTHE GAMBRELL
LIBRARY

Jacqulin Bennett

In Memory
of Christa
McAuliffe

Megan
Phillips

The Question & Answer Book

ALL ABOUT RIVERS

ALL ABOUT RIVERS

By Jane Emil
Illustrated by Joseph Veno

Troll Associates

Library of Congress Cataloging in Publication Data

Emil, Jane.
  All about rivers.

   (Question and answer book)
   Summary: Answers questions about the formation and
development of rivers, differences among rivers, and
the influence of rivers on human life.
    1. Rivers—Juvenile literature. [1. Rivers.
2. Questions and answers] I. Veno, Joseph, ill.
II. Title. III. Series: Question and answer book.
GB1203.8.E45 1984   551.48'3   83-4868
ISBN 0-89375-979-1
ISBN 0-89375-980-5 (pbk.)

How does a river begin?

A river begins its life in a small way.

It may start as a trickle of sparkling water fed by a cold mountain spring. Leaping over rocks and small cliffs, it tumbles down the mountainside. In the spring, snow on the mountain melts, and rain falls.

Now the trickle becomes a stream —growing wider and flowing faster. Fish dart through its clear waters, as wild animals and birds stop to drink. Fine sand and small pebbles are swept along on the stream's downward journey.

Flowing toward the low land of the valley below, the stream is joined by other streams. Together, they become a large river. It spills into the valley in a broad, rushing flow. Strong and powerful, the river carves a path through the fertile green land. From side to side, the water curves through the valley like a long snake.

Restless and always moving, the mighty river finally flows to the sea.

How are all rivers alike?

Not all rivers are large and power-ful enough to be called "mighty." Rivers come in all sizes. But long or short, wide or narrow, all rivers are natural bodies of flowing water. They flow in paths called *channels*, or *riverbeds*. The streams that flow into a river are called its branches, or *tributaries*. A river and its tributaries are known as a *river system*.

How many names do rivers have?

Rivers have many names—*streams*, *brooks*, *creeks*. Very small streams are often called *rills* or *runnels*. The land through which a river flows is a *river valley*.

What is a river's source?

Rivers are formed by water that stays on the surface of the land and flows downhill. Many rivers begin high in snow-filled mountains. The beginning of a river is called its *source*, or *headwaters*. Even the mightiest rivers have very small beginnings.

What is the longest river?

The world's longest river is the Nile in Egypt. It is 4,160 miles (6,656 kilometers) long. The Nile flows northward and is made up of three main branches. Its southern source, the White Nile, begins in the highlands of a small African nation. The Blue Nile and the Atbara, joining the Nile further north, are thought to start in a mountain spring.

What is the widest river?

The Amazon, in South America, is the world's widest river. It is also the second longest river. It has hundreds of tributaries, and it carries more water than any other river in the world. The Amazon is so wide in some places that you cannot see from one shore to the other. But even this great river starts as a small stream high in the mountains of Peru.

AMAZON

WOW!

What is the longest river in North America?

The Mississippi and Missouri rivers in the United States are usually counted as one river system. This river system is the third longest in the world—almost as long as the Amazon. Although this big river system is called the Mississippi, geographers say that the Missouri River is really the main river.

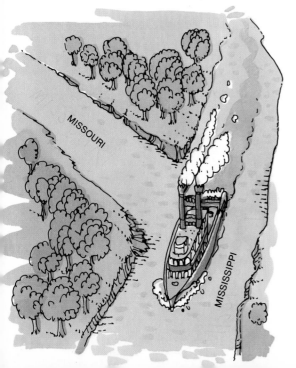

MISSOURI

MISSISSIPPI

9

How does a glacier become part of a river?

A mountain glacier is a great mass of moving ice. It forms where the air is very cold—so cold that most ice never melts. Layer upon layer of snow falls and freezes. Finally, the weight of this ice mass becomes so great that it begins to slide downhill. Most glaciers don't slide very fast—probably just a few inches a day.

If the front edge of a glacier slides into warmer air, some of it melts. The cold glacial water may form its own mountain stream, or it may flow into another stream and become part of a river.

Can a glacier block a flowing river?

Yes. Sometimes a glacier may slide right into the path of a flowing river. If the glacier blocks the river channel, the river must change course. In the state of Washington, the Columbia River carved out a new channel after a glacier blocked the old one a long, long time ago. The old, empty channel, which is called the Grand Coulee, can still be seen.

What is a river's drainage basin?

Water that falls on the land around a river will flow, or drain, into that river. This land is called a river's *drainage basin*. Rivers are often measured by the size of their drainage basins. The Amazon River has the largest drainage basin. It is nearly two-thirds as large as the whole United States! Waters from six countries in South America drain into the Amazon.

The drainage basin of the Mississippi includes about one-third of the United States. Waters from thirty-one states and two provinces in Canada find their way into the Mississippi system.

What is the Continental Divide?

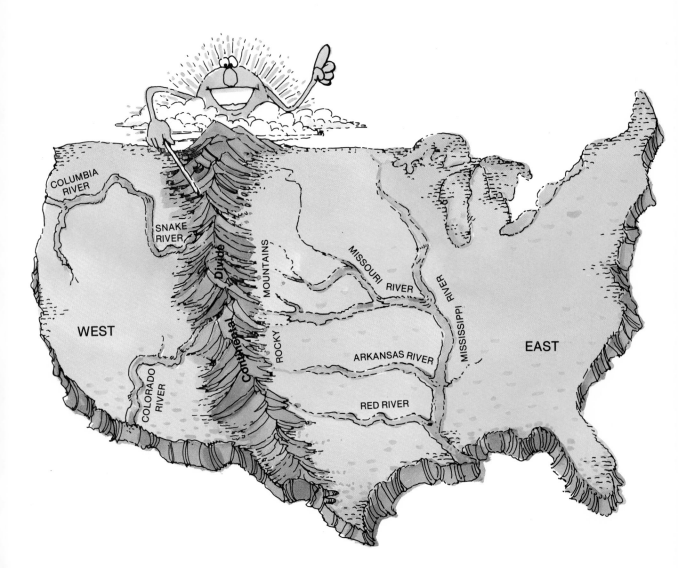

Streams that are east of the *crest*, or highest point, of the Rocky Mountains flow into the Mississippi. Streams west of the crest send their waters to the Snake, Columbia, Colorado, and other western rivers. This crest line between the streams that drain to the east and west is called the *Continental Divide*.

What do rivers look like from above?

If you could look down upon the Mississippi drainage basin from high in the sky, you would see a tree-like pattern. The Mississippi flows down from the north. The Missouri flows eastward from the Rockies. The two rivers join near the middle of the country. They form one huge "tree trunk." Branches of all sizes join the trunk along its course. The entire drainage basin looks like a tree with many arms. This tree-like pattern is the most common river-basin pattern.

Some river basins have a pattern that looks like a winding maze. The force of the water, flowing in and out of the basin, builds a maze of ridges and valleys.

How do rivers lose water?

Rivers receive water, but they lose it, too. Hot sun and dry air help to evaporate, or dry up, a lot of the water that rivers carry. Yet some rivers get so much water at their source that they can cross large deserts without going dry. The Nile and the Colorado both cross deserts before spilling into the sea.

14

What is a waterfall?

On its way to the sea, a river may tumble over a cliff or steep drop. This is called a *waterfall*. Sometimes a river drops in a series of water-falls. This is called a *cascade*. Some-times a river flows swiftly downhill over many rocks. These places are known as *rapids*.

What is erosion?

Day after day, year after year—now faster, now slower, but never stopping—a river flows from its source to the sea. Its rushing water carries along bits of soil and rock called *sediment*. The sediment and the force of the water wear away the land. This is called *erosion*. Given enough time, a river can change the earth in amazing ways.

How can a river change the earth?

One example of a river that has changed the earth is the Niagara River, which flows between two of the Great Lakes—Lake Erie and Lake Ontario. About midway in its course, the river spills over a high cliff. This spectacular drop is called Niagara Falls. Over the centuries, the powerful Niagara River has eroded the limestone rock of the cliff. The force of the water is so great that the Falls have been cut back more than 7 miles (11 kilometers) from where they began!

But not even the Niagara can match the work of the Colorado River. Over millions of years, the Colorado has carved through layer after layer of many-colored rock in northwestern Arizona. It has cut a deep slash that is 250 miles (400 kilometers) long. It is from 4 to 18 miles (6.5 to 29 kilometers) wide. This is the awesome and beautiful Grand Canyon. Looking out over the land, it is hard to believe that a river could have carved such a huge canyon.

What are the "ages" of a river?

Like most things on the earth, rivers change through the years. A river has three ages—young, mature, and old. These words are used to describe how the river looks.

What is a young river?

A *young* river usually has steep, high banks, and its course is fairly straight. A young river may flow very fast, often through rapids and over waterfalls.

19

What is a mature river?

The banks of a *mature* river are not so steep or high.
The flow of water is slower. Rapids and waterfalls are
worn down. The river carries soil, mud, and fine sand
called *silt*. The Missouri River dumps a good deal of silt
into the Mississippi. That is why the Missouri is often
called the "Big Muddy."

What is an old river?

Erosion has been at work for a long time on an *old* river. The banks have become gentle slopes. The river flows slowly through a wide, flat valley. A slow-flowing river does not have the power to carve deeply into the land. Instead, the river tends to *meander*, wandering in lazy curves across a flat plain.

A long river can be young, mature, and old all at the same time. The Mississippi looks young at its source and mature in the middle of its course. But it is an old river when it reaches the Gulf of Mexico.

What is the mouth of a river?

The place where a river meets a large body of water is called the river's *mouth*. Most rivers spill into oceans or seas.

What is a delta?

At the end of its journey, a river drops the sediment it has carried. The river pushes the sediment out, forming land that is called a *delta*. Most deltas look like big, sandy fan-like triangles.

Building a delta is a sort of never-ending contest between the ocean and the river. The river keeps pushing the sediment out into the ocean. The ocean keeps washing some of it back. That's why river deltas are always changing.

Deltas are some of the world's best farming areas. But some, like the Nile's delta, are also filled with salty lakes and swampy land. Others, like the delta of the Ganges River in India, are crazy-quilt patterns made by many constantly changing streams. The huge Mississippi delta changes, too. This river adds about 6 miles (9.6 kilometers) of new land to its delta every century.

What is an estuary?

Instead of building a delta, some rivers scoop out the land when they reach the sea. The sea tides flow into the mouth of the river. This scooped-out mouth is called an *estuary*. Estuaries make fine harbors. The estuary of the Hudson River forms New York City's harbor.

How do rivers help us?

Rivers help us in many ways. Two of the most important things they give us are water to drink and fish to eat. Rivers also are a source of rich farmland, and they provide water for crops.

People have always settled near rivers, and they still do. One of the reasons is because rivers give us the means of transportation needed for carrying out trade.

A river's waterfalls can provide us with great amounts of energy. And certain rivers have important minerals in their riverbeds, such as quartz and gold.

But best of all, rivers give us their beauty. A river can be the perfect place for all kinds of recreation, including swimming, boating, and fishing.

Can rivers be dangerous?

You can see the power of a river when you look at the Grand Canyon. Or when you watch the water tumbling in great foamy sprays over Niagara Falls. But never is a river's power so awesome, so frightening, and so terrible as during a *flood.*

When a river floods, it spills over its banks and spreads across the land. Houses and people can be swept away by the force of a river running wild.

Every year there are floods in some parts of the world. Rivers are most likely to flood in the spring, when rain and melting snow increase the amount of water in their channels. Floods cause terrible damage. One of the worst floods in history happened about a hundred years ago on China's Yellow, or Hwang Ho, River. Nearly a million people died. More recently, the Arno River in Italy flooded the city of Florence, which is famous for its art collections. Paintings from centuries past were destroyed in just a few hours.

In the past, the Mississippi and the Nile often flooded. Spring floods ruined good farmland and wiped out homes and towns. The damage was terrible and costly. But today these rivers have been brought somewhat under control.

How can we stop floods?

There is no way to stop *all* floods. But there is a way to stop some floods and to lessen the damage of others. It is called *flood control*.

One method of flood control is to build high banks, called *levees*, along a river. The levees keep the rising water in its channel. Another way is to scoop out and deepen the river channel with big digging machines. A deeper channel will hold more water. Sometimes extra channels are dug next to the main channel. The flood water runs into the channels instead of over the land.

Dams are built on some rivers to control the water flow. They store extra water in specially created lakes called *reservoirs*. When the water begins to rise and there is danger of flooding, the extra water can be held in the reservoir. When the flood danger is past, the water in the reservoir is allowed to flow back into the river.

You can see levee after levee on the flat land of the lower Mississippi River. Some levees are as high as a two-story house! And there are dams and reservoirs along the entire river system. On the Nile, the huge Aswan High Dam holds back flooding water. It also creates electric power and stores water for crops. So much water is held behind the dam that it has backed up into a lake that is 300 miles (480 kilometers) long!

One of the world's most famous flood control projects is on the Tennessee River in the south-central United States. The Tennessee River is only about 650 miles (1,040 kilometers) long. But at one time it created as much trouble as a river ten times its length. The Tennessee was always in flood. Farmland was ruined every year. Forests were destroyed. Homes were washed away. Something had to be done.

So the Tennessee Valley Authority, or TVA, was created in 1933. With the TVA, flood control came to the Tennessee Valley. Today there are many dams on the river. Reservoirs behind the dams store extra water during flood season. The Tennessee River has become a chain of lakes connected by the dams. The dams also bring electric power to the valley.

Why should we keep our rivers clean?

Not long ago, many people thought that we would always have clean water—no matter what we did to make it dirty. Now we know that isn't true. We now know that water is more precious than gold.

So people everywhere are taking a new look at our rivers in an effort to keep them clean. We need our rivers healthy. We need the great falls of foaming water that bring us electric power. We need the clear, sparkling mountain streams full of darting fish. We need small gurgling springs and wide, lazy rivers, making their never-ending journey to the sea. For whether large or small, flowing quickly or slowly, a river is one of nature's marvelous and special wonders.